Babylon

Poems by Jeffrey L. Johnson

Fernwood
PRESS

Babylon
©2023 by Jeffrey L. Johnson

Fernwood Press
Newberg, Oregon
www.fernwoodpress.com

All rights reserved. No part may be reproduced for any commercial purpose by any method without permission in writing from the copyright holder.

Printed in the United States of America

Cover and page design: Mareesa Fawver Moss

Cover photo: Molly Porter

ISBN 978-1-59498-111-1

And here, for the first time in my life,
I saw my beloved Mississippi River.

—Jack Kerouac, *On the Road*

Are we perhaps here
to say: house, bridge, fountain, gate, pitcher,
fruit tree, window—at most, pillar, tower?
but to say them, you understand—
to say them in a way that even the things
themselves never thought to be so intimately.

—Rainer Maria Rilke, *Duino Elegies*

The image, in its simplicity, has no need of scholarship.
It is the property of a naïve consciousness;
in its expression it is youthful language.

—Gaston Bachelard, *The Poetics of Space*

Give sorrow words. The grief that does not speak
Whispers the o'er fraught heart and bids it break.

—Shakespeare, *Macbeth*

Contents

Sovereign 9
Swiping a Lunch 10
For the Boys of Gaza 11
Every Stone Shall Cry 12
Prophet 14
Northfield Bank Raid 16
Bird Art 17
VFW USA 18
1863 19
Sunday Afternoon 20
Religion in America 21
Saviors 22
Love Thy Neighbor 23
Good Night 24
Weekend 25
Dressed in Holiday Style 26
Nunc Dimittis 27
Winter Green 28
Cheeseburger Smiles 29
Blessed Assurance 30
Morning Snow 31
Rocking 32

Remembering Father Louis 33
Pushing Off 34
Order for Burial 35
    I. Visitation 35
    II. Elegy 36
    III. Benediction 37
    IV. Committal 38
    V. Reception 39
Remember Sabbath 40
School Closings 41
Passages 42
Almost Sixty 43
Middle Age 44
When You Get Out of the House 45
Born into Lunch 46
Come Back Here, Boy 47
Joy to the World 48
Good Question 49
Boo, Daddy! 50
Stay 51
Morning Reading 52
Knuckles of God 53
Reading Old Jerusalem 54
Mark's Short Ending 55
Easter Vigil 56
Babylon 57
I'll Pick You Up 58
Patriarch 59
On the Deck 60
Gettysburg 61
Commencement 62
Inheritance 63
After All 64
A Tale for Children 65
Question for an Exile 68
Title Index 69
First Line Index 73

Babylon

Sovereign

My neighbor's rooster reigns all day,
crowing dominion
over the hens' undertones of hope.

When loneliness weakens the legs
and excites the eyes
to find a way out of confinement

and no escape is located, then
all that's left are spells of shamans,
guidance from yogis,

playlists of gurus, incantations of priests,
commentaries by social scientists
on patterns of rush-hour traffic

and reasons for the behavior
of a middle-age man, seen earlier,
strutting in the sun

after a big restaurant lunch:
shoulders back, belly spilling out,
teeth splintering a toothpick to prove

his daylight hours are leisure
and that, if he chose to, he could puff
his chest and crow bluster to the sun.

Swiping a Lunch

Humble enough to hold a parable
together, a brown-bag lunch
left by a mom in service

of her master, time, became mine
when I unrolled the top reverently,
unfolded waxed paper

around the sandwich—a swipe
of peanut butter and a swipe
of jelly on a slice of white bread,

cut on the diagonal.
Four thin carrot sticks
to bend and break, an eight-ounce

water to chug in four swallows,
and—eyes closed in respect
of childhoods, hers and mine,

and in honor of childhoods
she must have been shaping—
four bites of a Fun Size Snickers.

For the Boys of Gaza

Tire smoke and tear gas
incense your faces
and infect your breath
when you rise together
as blood brothers,
boiling from damp alleys
where defiance seeps
through unscheduled days,
hydrating your brains
enough to sprout an idea
for employment: Why not
harvest fist-size desert fruit,
whip them one by one
at foreign windshields
and door panels?
When hours of rest fall,
blood smears your fingers
and dries on your bony wrists.
Pain settles with sacrifices
poverty has forced on you,
as the blushing sun buries
its face in the softness
of the hills and hides
in the lap of the mindful sea.

Every Stone Shall Cry

I don't remember much
about my childhood
except that the stones
would not shut up.

I know now that rocks
press through earth
everywhere, turn to soil
for planting crops,

to bricks for building
homes, to mud on boots
of soldiers, dust on
skin of the invisible poor.

I don't remember much
about my childhood
except that rocks shouted
louder than threats

bouncing off stone-walled
alleys of Jerusalem,
echoing loud as warnings
in fields around Bethlehem.

I do remember my sister,
frozen in a gas mask,
and I, beside her,
bent to a transistor radio

behind taped windows
when sirens screamed
and stones exploded
with voices like a mob.

I don't remember much
about my childhood
except the rocks that sang
from chisels on the temple

as portends of war washed
the holy city in water
and blood, and my father
snapped at my mother

before he touched
her face and closed
his eyes so those
loud-as-hell stones

would finally quiet
down, so he could try
tenderness without
all that racket around.

Prophet

Eat this scroll and speak
to the house of Israel;
see this vision and dance
for exhausted exiles;

hold my hand and lead
the wandering children
out of slavery toward
land prepared for them.

They will arrive by-and-by,
but you must go back
to the word and eat it
together with your tears.

Be satisfied, prophet,
with the words I give you
and with meditations
of your heavy heart.

Be fed by the hunger
within you; swallow my
word, and a loaf will become
as a pounding stone to you.

Run the edge of a sharp
sword across your scalp.
Divide the shavings between
a fire and the wind.

March to Mount Zion,
my holy hill, and there
raise your loudest voice
to accelerate my anger.

Assemble my children
with the sound of singing;
tell them my fury over
the evil of their days.

Clap your hands and stamp
your feet, prophet.
Splash their idols with your
breath and warn that

mountains of gold are not
sufficient ransom.
Chariots will not save
the people from my word

because my word is a vacuum
that draws the cherub
messengers to the wind,
with the glory of my house.

As you go, prophet,
I promise to send
a companion, an affliction
for your weary way:

a thorn in your side shall
remain with you, I promise.
You shall pray for pain—
your only friend—to stay.

Northfield Bank Raid

All the boys wanted that day
was help with their masks,
so they could find or buy
somewhere the kind of life

kept safe and fair by rule
of straps and bruises, but
when the money ran out
again, Jesse spurred a stolen

horse up Main ahead of his
straggle of bearded boys
in white dusters cut long
enough to cover .45's

that fathers they didn't have
would have made them drop
before they played out
their howl of a plan in the sun,

for families to recall years
later, with carnivals, cotton
candy, clowns, and police cars
ahead of marching bands.

Bird Art

Here, even this beggar
in front of my car
may hop up to mustard
on swordfish skin,
gristle on porkchops,
gray-on-green orange peels,
brown wilted lettuce.
A one-legged seagull's
dreamscape, every day
serving remnants
of kitchen and yard
in black plastic bags
and smeared newsprint.
What method maimed
this unfortunate diner
at his midday buffet?
Hooked beak of a brother?
Sharp clamp of a lover?
Severe barking bite
of a gray outlaw stranger?
Wet snap of a bluefish
thrashing below,
finding little to like
on that leathery claw?
Rocks from a sunbather
grown edgy and mean
in unblinking anger,
glaring down at noon
on a scavenger cadger?

VFW USA

Near Okinawa I saw
Japanese soldiers on fire.
They held their hands
high over torches of hair
our boys took for targets.

I saw a big British soldier
clean house with sledges
bound to serve his queen:
crack an enlisted nose
and shake Allied hands.

I saw Butch catch an apple
near his navel, lose his middle
somewhere around Saigon
where they still run and run
for cover, away from

the city, in old movie loops,
through stories told over
and over by men swimming
in place in beer, back
through unplanned tours.

1863

Wrapped in wool, with no other
place in the world to go,
they rode steerage for Ellis Island.

Two nights from Stavanger
they passed through a bawl
of a preserving salt spray.

Landed, they knocked away on rails
for Chicago, then rolled day after
day on wagons for Dakota.

They rode out their first Christmas
in a blizzard blowing down
blindness for Rosy.

When Rosy's hundred-pound
boulder of a head fell, the courtesy
of winter shrouded the carcass.

A spring wagon train chipped
uncovered ox flesh like green hickory
for frying on their fire.

All the way out to Dakota,
one woman looked back through grass
that sprang from the wheels.

The grass said *shu-ah* under the clap
of the sky, the same damn thing
aloud in her head: *Come ahead,*

past the next tuft of prairie;
there'll be a home for your heart,
dear. Shu-ah, shu-ah.

Sunday Afternoon

Music of America covers
the stuck-record statements
residents mumble and repeat
around star-spangled tables.

A woman coos to the bald head
of a doll across her arms.
Another woman hums,
I love you, I love you,

as she strokes the sweater
of a man asleep beside her.
Another woman holds Rollo,
a white and liver spaniel.

I wonder if any of them dream
of fish eyes, as I am now,
of bluegills flopping like glitter;
of pike, wild and green

on the bottom of the boat;
of walleyes, olive and gold,
their big eyes invaluable.

Religion in America

Numbers and statistics sorted
and stacked like cordwood
accelerate fires
along the valley of dry bones.

Studies pile facts like bricks
scrubbed and rinsed in a slurry
of crushed rocks of ages,
and cornerstones rejected

become figures, certified,
catalogued, and archived
with dates of diminishments
and extinctions noted.

Then a spirit stirs a touch,
and a kiss of a baby's breath
on a grandparent's cheek,
raises wishes for whispers

in assembly, for hope to bow
to morning showers, for uncanny
words to breathe through
branches of family trees.

Saviors

When your head was high
as your knees are now,
helpers who joined you
at trains or stacking blocks,
adults who restored balance,
lifted you when you toddled
and fell; they are your messiahs,
standing by with the saints
to step forward in peace again
when you bend for a pencil
or fumble for keys, when a leg
of your walker snags
the corner of a throw rug.
That's when you need them,
and that's when they'll come.

Love Thy Neighbor

In slow motion,
hinged legs hook
wires deliberately;
a feathery mouth-
piece and donkey-
ear antennae test
every even space
between the wires;
the sting at the end
of the abdomen
probes and tries
perfect squares
of nothing but air
and patiently holds
its pinch of fire.

Good Night

Engines grind from a shoal
where my resident ship
is jammed in the shallows.

Inky-sounding sprays of water
discharge in rhythmic lurches:
a tug chomping to float it free
or release it to open ocean.

I awake, turn, and submit again
to a play of unexpected faces
in bays of eccentric places.

Weekend

There will be bonsai trees
trimmed and blossomed in air;

periwinkles sparkling, twirling,
drilling sun-sprinkled sand;

loons arriving Saturday, *who-whoodle-
who*, expecting, as they always do,

red roses in black vases, caviar on
crackers, violins, and a singer.

And if none of that, then release
of a branch from its sponsoring trunk

where it softened unnoticed to an
untrustworthy display for the seasons;

a lawnmower blade scalping crowns
from a mole's network of tunnels;

a blue jay swanking on a feeder
after bombing titmice and chickadees.

Dressed in Holiday Style

Visitors squeezed past a family
gathered around a child who held
a holiday diorama in her hands.
When a string of lemon lights
let go in the jostle, the huddle
of faces turned to watch lemon
drops tick off shoes to vinyl tiles.
A teacher appeared, picked up
a candy and told how her student
skipped recess to glue glitter;
scoured for days to find frosted pines,
colored balls, silver tinsel, foil-
wrapped presents, candy canes,
and fur-trimmed elves in red knit
caps and black boots; skipped lunch
one day to hang *Deck the Halls*;
came in early another day to place
reindeer hooves securely in cotton
snow, to trim the edges with plastic
holly sprigs, make it all ring.

Nunc Dimittis

A nor'easter arrived at sunset
as dinner was served
in a windowless basement

in honor of an Armenian bishop
who spoke of the saints
as if they were his uncles.

The woman next to me wore
a sweater-dress the color of coal,
had short gray hair, skin

the color of chocolate ice cream,
and a bottom as big
as a bushel basket on the chair.

Over eclairs and coffee
she told me that if I doubted
there was evil, I should study war.

In the dark, snow scrubbed up
sabbath and dressed our houses
in bunting like a blessing.

Inside my house I waited
for the weather on Channel 7,
then in peace erased the morning

schedule and took a holiday place
to sing in a day of rest with songs
in four parts at the piano.

Winter Green

We rein a toboggan down banks
to ice whipped up in swirls,
buckled to impossible peaks.

Falling back on quilted hoods,
we wait for blossoming stars
to show on a twilight canvas,

for late sparkles to appear to us
like the clematis flowers do
when we're sure summer's over.

Cheeseburger Smiles

In line behind a wooden fence rail,
three Tanzanian boys ham
for the loving eye of a camera.

The tallest's gap-tooth smile,
orbed forehead, and shaved skull
remind me of my little brother,

the way he smiled when our father
focused his Polaroid on us
and said, *Say cheeseburger, boys!*

The eyes of the elder who said that,
his scent behind the camera, are gone,
but they break back to me

from these faces, smiling for love
and a tax-deductible donation
in a noon-flash near Bukoba.

Blessed Assurance

We're happier than we deserve to be.
Did you ever think of it that way?

In the lobby, hair combed, shoes shined,
we're ready for the matinee performance.

Later, eyes wide, legs colt-fresh, we'll step
out to rain-wash atomizing streetlight

shine and headlight beams across
a star-scoured moon-polished night stage,

spread without direction and without
end, in desire wider than our imaginations.

Morning Snow

The sun appeared to say
that snow cannot stay

in the air while a man grows
into his office in life.

After all, his is ordinary
time, not a flurry in the eyes

of a child out of school
with mittens and a *Flexible Flyer*.

Snowflakes fall from silver
sources, spend their lives

in play and ecstatic communion
until, against dead weight

of earth, they repose,
faces fast against faces.

Rocking

Perry Como, cool
as a sophomore beside
a piano, has been a guest
in my house forever,
he and his friends Cole
and Crosby, and Martin,
slurring words to cover
shame he hides in boxer's
hands, cupping a cigarette
or holding a bourbon.
There's Sinatra, of course.
But who's left to sing
through the after-hours
when Tony Bennett dies?
Not Andy Williams;
he's been gone a long time.
Not Steve and Eydie.
They're not around.

Remembering Father Louis

Two crew-cut monks,
one over eighty
in bedroom slippers,

the other past sixty
in Nike basketball shoes,
could pass for old coaches

except for their hickory-
boned, knot-knuckled hands.

In a deep-mine voice,
the older monk asks us
to imagine a hand.

It's easy to imagine it,
a working man's hand,
phalanges carved

and strung loosely.
Now, if you can, in that
hand, see a diamond.

This poor working man
knew the carat and cut
of light held in amazement.

*Father Louis was the name given to Thomas Merton
at his ordination as a Catholic priest.

Pushing Off

Beside being a way
for a man to kill time,
fishing is of value to a boy
who wants to study
his grandfather's hands.

Threading a line
through the eye of a hook,
a rich man can show
his grandson to fish
in less time than it takes
to call on the name of God;

snapping leaders,
tying flies, untangling snags,
managing a landing
in front of grandsons
who are pleased to know
what their elder can do.

If he cannot drive a plow,
turn a lathe, or plumb a wall,
at least he can snap
split-shots above a swivel
to punctuate a blue line
that leads to a silver spoon.

Order for Burial

I. Visitation

A long time passed without a word
from me, a sign to ponder, tracks

to follow, clicking keys, ink trails
folded, meant to message him.

I heard his baritone as snow-flake
soul-fall, barely anything at all,

when a hollow, drilled out
out of me, and he was ready to leave.

I would have known—a word would
have broken in me—if he had gone

from the ER or flown in his sleep.
I would have arrived in the evening

light to mourning doves telling who
he was and how well they knew him.

II. Elegy

Years after he left a prairie town
where his father trucked cattle

and stored grain, early-morning
cartoons chittered as his son steadied

sauce pans of boiling water, sterilizing
insulin syringes through the living

room, up three stairs, football pajama
legs juking drops that fell like flames

of suffering on bare feet: obedience
melting tenderness, throat catching

sparks that nicked and rusted like
scars on the frame of the old bike.

III. Benediction

Blessed were you, third toe,
obedient good soldier in line.

In your mother's rinse rhyme,
you had roast beef every time.

We hardly recall, but you must
have been shy, no trouble at all.

We loved you, of course, toe.
We don't miss you much though,

not you alone but you and the
whole body that left us by slivers.

IV. Committal

Carry the kids in from the wagon
through chirping summer darkness.

Tuck them under clown sheets;
wake them with the sun and bacon.

Punt a football high as the crown
of the patriarch silver maple.

Push off in your hockey skates again,
ankles holding on smooth blue ice.

The town's huddled in for you.
Its streets and venues are all yours.

V. Reception

A toast to a graceful retreat for him
to family-room highlights and reruns,

to cracking scrapbook snapshots or
logy farewell trivia of do-you-remember.

If he could have stopped the heart pills,
poured out the insulin, been quick when

a dam blocked an artery, we would have
missed the heart re-piped, plasma leaking

through veins turned to pulp, eyes clouded
by cataracts, kidneys occluded by time.

Remember Sabbath

Keep it holy,
as you recall slavery
in Pharaoh's brickyard
before the Lord broke
the lock and dropped you
in freedom on the bank
of a river sluicing
thin streams for sprouts
waiting patiently in line.
Snowy Sundays,
dozing with sports pages
spread on your chest,
push off from a dock, set
on ages of Egyptian rocks,
for promised Canaan.
Click back in your recliner
for football; recall your
people who kept it
like that, same as you do.

School Closings

On a runway to pileups
at the coasts, the ancient
prairie flashes mirages where
earth bends toward romantic
plains and western fabrications.

If you let your eyes wander
across a map, you might
beat out a spill of trochees,
train-stop seeds dropped
along wagon trails west.

Call out the towns
in a radio voice as if drifts
from an overnight blizzard
block the highways: Clements,
Cobden, Comfrey, Darfur,

Essig, Morgan, Morton,
Fairfax, Sanborn, Westbrook,
Tracy, Dotson, crumbled quorums,
each one home to a handful
trying to rise above the weather.

Passages

Yup'ik boys lay
their first killed seals
at the feet of old
women of the village.
Fur and fat, meat
and innards deliver
calories to the families
and to the dogs,
and keep the women's
hands occupied
with their stitching.
My brother and I
knocked down four
bluebills and an out-
of-season canvasback,
a red-headed prince,
down on a whim from
a northern flyway.
We laid the carcasses
together on the deck
of the cabin where
Grandmother sewed in
the sun: my goodness,
boys, look at these.

Almost Sixty

The camel train bogged down
in sandstorms more than once,
folded in place, set off again.

Past is the time for turning
back to the star's crystal rings
of sand-frost and smoke-fog,

birth gifts of an old friend,
the snow prince, at home
in my chest, head in the sky,

feet flat on Jordan's hard-pack.
Freedom is thick in the air.
The reins have been handed off.

Tracks are trails across still water.
Colored eggs have all been found.
Epiphanies disappear overnight.

Middle Age

Membranes, too porous
to block out the blight
of years, absorb infections
and dissolve them
in a molecular dance:
shoving, sidling to a blue
pull of music recorded
for recalling the order
of seating, Christmas Eve,
twenty-five years ago.
Cataracts have appeared,
flake on a globe, fleck
on a lens-turning-to-bark,
deadening the memory
of a week at the lake
when a woodpecker
wouldn't stop knocking
at dawn, so no one slept in.

When You Get Out of the House

Drive north on two-twelve
to Deep Portage Road, then
sixteen miles west to White Earth
Lake Lodge on Battleground Point.

Bear will be waiting, but please
don't feed Bear a bite of your
sandwich or, for goodness' sake,
not a square of teeth-rotting Hershey.

No wake through the outlet. Outside
the jetty, past the buoys, you can
open it up, south south/west, if you're
lucky, into the teeth of the wind.

Under an overcast sky and on stiff
chop, you might see a Goldeneye
drake drop in and slide-plow a few
yards through steely green ripples.

It's thirteen to fifteen feet down
to sand bottom, north of Mule Island,
a hundred yards out from the eagle's nest.
Troll up, drift back over the drop-off.

The drake will turn his face to the wind,
for mist on his bill and his pompadour.
That duck's not too old for a day out
of touch, on the water, in the weather.

Born into Lunch

Lining up to settle accounts
with Sue of blue apron: Thank you.

We pay, pass through, and one
by one are born into lunch in the sun.

With both hands Sue's children bear
choices on nicked, clownish trays;

smiling fortunates are born shoulder
to shielding shoulder with others.

Tall rays of noon shine down on us all.
How do you do? If no friend appears

to shade and console, one is surely
nearby, gone ahead or in line.

Come Back Here, Boy

Corky wasn't bathed much
except for a few times with
V8 when a loitering skunk
he cornered at sunset
unloaded straight in his face.

He crashed through corn rows
for scented bumpers.
When roaming town dogs
crossed the property line,
Corky came out like a shot.

He had an old paint tray
for pellets, ice-cream pails
warmed with green film
in summer and cracking to
bullying ice in winter.

Quilts piled in the corner
of the garage were a bed.
When arthritis set in, his
oily hide stank, flies bit the
soft skin of his ears, turning

them leathery black, pin-
dropped with blood. Eyelids,
red crescents from twelve,
thirteen years, pooled tears
of the best dog of my life.

Joy to the World

When our baby wakes
on Christmas Day,
I touch his smooth cheek
with my lips and look in
on his tongue testing
the tops of the walls
of pink gum lines.

I cradle his siren
and let the screams pile
to an ache in my ear.

We cannot say what
we mean by these pains,
so I hand him over,
and she, full and round,
feeds our liquid blue eyes,
all four unacquainted
with light waking up
to yawn over the snow.

Good Question

*If you ate a whole cake,
could you fix a rainy day?*

I believe I could fix it
if the cake was light
as the air was that day
we poked around
off the dock with a net
and an old canoe oar.

I believe I could fix it
if the frosting was smooth
as light reflecting off
the moon that night
when a bear came by,
disguised as a baker,

to deliver cakes to the door
of our tent: one for you
to eat next to me, one
for me to eat while we
retold our old stories
and stirred up new ones.

Boo, Daddy!

Were you scared, or would you like
to make chocolate-chip pancakes?

My new gopher jumped out of his bed
and onto the floor last night.

I thought I made a good place for him
with cotton balls in the shoe box you found.

I colored it all over with crayons.
Blue inside, red outside. You helped.

Stay

They lunge at their chains,
shake out soft-mouth, wag-tail
routines, break free, bolt off
into the night for as long
as the darkness will have them.

They've nosed around for years,
accepted pats for counsel
and obedience at bedside,
for service spreading crumbs
to satisfy the well-fed.

Collared, gray-eyed, sunburned
from days without end
in the spray of the word, older
ones lope tree-to-tree through
shifting shadows of their master.

Misery lodges in their throats;
fog from the gospel drips
off their hides; their blood boils
from a dream that the summoning
hand falls on them again, cooling

their soul-melt, picking up
their blame, then, aiming a greased
claw, cuts veined valleys for them
to explore with fires set to light
their way through the woods.

Morning Reading

Mustard seeds, a new father
needs a word from you.
Gloria in excelsis Deo will do
until the story drifts from Galilee
back to Judea, as it always does.

For now the father needs help
digging ordinary furrows,
deep and true, plow-lines
for litanies to sprout straight,
and mounds for fig trees to rise

from fire-blanched ground, in
soil for red grapes to swell blue,
and for specks like you—seeds—
to explode sun-burst shade
and promised shelter above him.

Knuckles of God

A white-robed Bedouin
ushers us through
dry rivulet, mountain
pass, wadi, and highway
worn dear to his eyes
as the back of his
chocolate brown hand
on the wheel of a
dust-blasted 4Runner.
Skin sandstone, blood
copper, black granite
tuck to almighty fists
that steer too much law
and awe everlasting
to our lives, so we roll
out a dust cloud
and race to the side
of that old joker, the sea.

Reading Old Jerusalem

A White Father skims French devotions
under Anne's outstretched arms.
A lady in blue lifts an Anglican hymn

to those arms, reinforced to hold
quiet repetitions and wobbly renditions
like theirs, in sacred relief.

Siblings are born of St. Anne's invitation.
She says, come again, dears. Sing
of your home in my heart; I'll give back

double and more in return; my arms,
cooled and uplifted, are spread for
your words: I catch them and keep them all.

Black-robed Copts, bearded heads bobbing,
read on a roof, a hot raft in the sunshine.
Their reading, like fishing, can go on all day.

Under protest of Babel, we slip into chambers
where languages glitter like baubles.
A Greek brother dozes, laid out on a chair

in the tomb of our Lord. Could you not wake
to greet children lined up to see nothing?
Snoring betrays your limp body.

Mark's Short Ending

We heard the angel's stiff clarion: *Go on,
tell Peter!* We'd rather go back to bed,
pull woolen blankets over our heads,
without boiling tea, and dream it away.

Peter's a red-headed wild bull of the vale.
His beard is a tangle of briars in the fire.
His eyes are embers that pop in the hot part,
frightening children like cat-o'-nine tails.

His head is a mat of thick curled ram's wool,
rolled in red clay and dust down the hillside.
Go and tell Peter? What should we tell him?
That the tongue of the lion was smooth?

The sharp teeth were bloodstained and red?
How to explain it? Say there's nothing
to fear from the steel of Rome's spears?
That those terrible blades vanish to nothing?

What words should we use? What figures will do?
That we tasted wild honey, presented on gold
by bees themselves? The angels have every
word, so let angels find some to tell Peter.

Easter Vigil

Horse and rider thrown into the sea.
We hear the now-and-everlasting
rumbling, breaking toward us:
Christ, the sun, rising in sea-shine
on a stage of blood-row fields.

Blades, once pliant, now are brittle,
streaked with salt-spray from
the burn of time, waving edges set
for vengeance of the Lord and long-
expected word. Could that be the son

of a rich man? No, the son of the
righteous, rolling old ocean, whose
flood formed us, swallowed us,
now swells to bear us off with the sun,
past shriven increments of time.

Babylon

There is more than enough sadness
to go around, so some of us get up
and gather fuel for funeral fires
we stoke up and down the river banks.
In copper and wicker, we haul gray
ash for scrubbing earthen cookware
and cleansing our immortal souls.

Others, with a gift for it, rehearse
silence they feel beneath the sand,
under pastures and vineyards, above
earth's jumble and tin, rhythms
rebounding off the skin of a drum,
rippling to flood desert wadis and soak
the crevices of our human brains.

Eyes averted, heads bowed, hands
clasped behind their backs, they follow
the clop and ruffle of military parades
and holiday advancements, as others
patrol the valley floors, examine
dimpled shadows cast by foreign
mountains that rise, tilt, and slide aside.

I'll Pick You Up

Come back inside, boy,
his sister called
through the screen.
He's probably drunk.

The part in his hair
pointed forward;
the boy stood straight,
waiting for his father,

for blue and gold lights
from the dashboard,
for popcorn and a big
cola eye in the dark.

He could not picture
his father in a brine,
without a stray thought
of the 7:30 show.

The dripper beeped,
clicked off time, days
and nights alike, sitting
large on four-dozen

and a handful more
years, with that night
still staring: stars
and moon sliding away

with the thought of never
again touching the hair
of a woman or standing
in the shred of cicadas.

Patriarch

November, and I miss steel sky
in a span above like a bowl
over old gold grass, conifers
supporting mounting snow,
earth bleeding sap and strength.

The Lord of November, a gray-
brown buck, hide thick for winter,
wide rack-crown slowing
the rise and turn of his great,
grazing head, appears on my lawn.

The deer sniffs for apples
and steps off through cedars
to scrub oaks, taking time toward
fallen chestnuts and forest seeds.
I watch him melt into wood.

No one hears the one-foot-next-foot
crackle he toes out on leaf-
papered ground or my voice
calling out to his broad back
without a start or a turn toward me.

On the Deck

Winter nights he honors us,
sitting out there patiently,
looking in through the glass,
long nose trembling,
bright eyes anticipating
lapping up offerings we set
out for him on plastic

because these are hard times
for salesmen and hunters
of small birds fallen from
mud-caked nests in the crooks
of trees, of mice in the grass.
Our parents remember hoboes
at chicken salad and blueberry

pie set out on picnic tables,
their faces washed in dust
thrown up between slats
into boxcars they rode through
the night, until first light
when they hunted for rest
in the arms of a family's trees.

Gettysburg

Steeds frozen to stone
near tasseled gold altars
honor blood spilled
in fountains and flows
poured from veins of lambs
strained through uniform
wool and out under hats
that made farm boys tall.

Imagine a narcotic night
coming on, the slightest
sounds cricking through
brains overloaded and numb;
cracks of betrayal, memory's
nettle, raking purple scars,
preceding public pounding
of history's displays.

The spirits of those whose
home fires were doused
rest between layers of air
sweetened by tourists'
menthol smoke and hotel
soap and chilled by ghosts
of lambs bleating all night,
all day: *blood shed for you.*

Commencement

If impractical thoughts
color your mind, go ahead,
spread them to the purifying air.

If you've found partners,
try to build something of gold
brick and blue steel.

If you stare into space a lot,
don't let street noise
and text messages distract you

from erasing red corrections,
stains on the horizon at evening.
These scratches remain

from teachings that brand brains,
such as that greed will save us
if only greed is tried.

If a plow appears before your eyes,
step up to that plow. It's yours.
Set your shoulders to it.

Grade, smooth, and straighten
wherever you can. Take sabbath rest
as sunshine and shade.

Inheritance

One of them got his hair
in its fullness, the splay
of his nose and the turn
of his jaw to his chin.

One seems to have won
the wreck of his humor
and the flat-footed width
of his horny beaten feet.

Every time his third child,
a daughter, smiles
at her baby when she coos,
the old guy shows up.

After All

Now that the world is flat,
wound around with wifi,
there's little hope of finding
trapdoors in the sod that
open with a cantillation on
a den of blue-hooded elves.

There's no more wonder
in buckshot stars blasting
a black sky of ignorance.

Connections are plugged in
properly, transmitting without
omens, tumbling in white
breakers or dancing on silver
feet under gray clouds swollen
purple, spilling out dreams.

A Tale for Children

On the shore of an ocean bay,
seafarers built boats of varnished oak
for shipping wool, grain, and lumber
to ports up and down the coast
and for fishing beyond the bay
for bearded cod and gray flounder.

Inland, in the distance, snow-capped
mountains towered to the clouds
behind carpets of green meadows.

Some of the seafarers migrated
to the meadows, where families
of shepherds tended flocks of sheep.
The shepherds cared for young lambs,
old ewes, and rams together.
They sheared sheep and packaged wool.

When the shepherds sat by the fire,
in the darkest nights of winter,
they remembered ancestor
seafarers, who fished for cod
and gray flounder and sailed up and down
the coast in boats made of oak.

As the shepherds tended flocks,
some of them dreamed of grasslands
that spread under the setting sun
on the other side of the mountains.

Some of them crossed the mountains
and learned to grow wheat and oats.
They built barns of stone and wood
and shipped grain away on steaming
trains across miles of prairie.

When the grain farmers sat by the fire,
in the darkest nights of winter,
they remembered ancestor shepherds,
who lived beside the mountains.

Some of the grain farmers moved
to apartments and houses built
side-by-side in the cities.
They worked in factories and stores.

When they sat by the fire,
in the darkest nights of winter,
they remembered ancestor
farmers, who lived on the prairie.

The city people worked long
hours in factories and stores.
Some of them bought automobiles
and moved to wooded suburbs, where
they built houses attached to large
garages surrounded by lawns.

In time, some of the suburban
children moved back to the city
or to homes with large garages
in suburbs of other cities.

When the families sat by the fire,
in the darkest nights of winter,
they remembered ancestors,
who lived in the city and worked
together in factories and stores.

The suburban families lived happily
for many years, caring for homes,
driving to malls and playgrounds.
A few of them dreamed of other places.

At dawn, on a winter day,
on the shore of a blue ocean bay,
people waved toward the sky
and watched a trail of light from a
rocket disappear above them.

They looked up and away and felt
strangely at home where they stood,
as if they had been on that shore
before, as if they could live there
again, or in the meadow beside
the mountains, or on the prairie,
or in a house on a city street.

Question for an Exile

If the spirit failed you, left you
without a plan or directions
to the father's house and riches
of his kingdom, would your friends
have gone on hale and hallelujah
healing and haranguing on behalf
of the poor broken-hearted even
as you faded, poor and broken-
hearted, yourself? Or let's say,
as you prayed, it dawned that you
could not return to Abba because
blessed-be-he had been dethroned
or, as the philosophers joked,
was dead. Then the lead taste and feel
that no one cared whether you walked
in or out or pounded dust around
Galilee on bare feet because
you left your sandals in Nazareth
would rise in your throat with the taste
of iron, and you would remember
that day as bitter, feel scars
spark and burn your back, wince
when you recalled the piercing thorns
bleeding out your fondest dreams.

Title Index

Symbols

1863 19

A

After All 64
Almost Sixty 43
A Tale for Children 65

B

Babylon 57
Benediction 37
Bird Art 17
Blessed Assurance 30
Boo, Daddy! 50
Born into Lunch 46

C

Cheeseburger Smiles 29
Come Back Here, Boy 47

Commencement 62
Committal 38

D

Dressed in Holiday Style 26

E

Easter Vigil 56
Elegy 36
Every Stone Shall Cry 12

F

For the Boys of Gaza 11

G

Gettysburg 61
Good Night 24
Good Question 49

I

I'll Pick You Up 58
Inheritance 63

J

Joy to the World 48

K

Knuckles of God 53

L

Love Thy Neighbor 23

M

Mark's Short Ending 55
Middle Age 44
Morning Reading 52
Morning Snow 31

N

Northfield Bank Raid 16
Nunc Dimittis 27

O

On the Deck 60
Order for Burial 35

P

Passages 42
Patriarch 59
Prophet 14
Pushing Off 34

Q

Question for an Exile 68

R

Reading Old Jerusalem 54
Reception 39
Religion in America 21
Remembering Father Louis 33
Remember Sabbath 40
Rocking 32

S

Saviors 22
School Closings 41
Sovereign 9
Stay 51
Sunday Afternoon 20
Swiping a Lunch 10

V

VFW USA 18
Visitation 35

W

Weekend 25
When You Get Out of the House 45
Winter Green 28

First Line Index

A

All the boys wanted that day 16
A long time passed without a word 35
A nor'easter arrived at sunset 27
A toast to a graceful retreat for him 39
A White Father skims French devotions 54
A white-robed Bedouin 53

B

Beside being a way 34
Blessed were you, third toe 37

C

Carry the kids in from the wagon 38
Come back inside, boy 58
Corky wasn't bathed much 47

D

Drive north on two-twelve 45

E

Eat this scroll and speak 14
Engines grind from a shoal 24

H

Here, even this beggar 17
Horse and rider thrown into the sea 56
Humble enough to hold a parable 10

I

I don't remember much 12
If impractical thoughts 62
If the spirit failed you, left you 68
If you ate a whole cake 49
In line behind a wooden fence rail 29
In slow motion 23

K

Keep it holy 40

L

Lining up to settle accounts 46

M

Membranes, too porous 44
Music of America covers 20
Mustard seeds, a new father 52
My neighbor's rooster reigns all day 9

N

Near Okinawa I saw 18
November, and I miss steel sky 59
Now that the world is flat 64
Numbers and statistics sorted 21

O

On a runway to pileups 41
One of them got his hair 63
On the shore of an ocean bay 65

P

Perry Como, cool 32

S

Steeds frozen to stone 61

T

The camel train bogged down 43
There is more than enough sadness 57
There will be bonsai trees 25
The sun appeared to say 31
They lunge at their chains 51
Tire smoke and tear gas 11
Two crew-cut monks 33

V

Visitors squeezed past a family 26

W

We heard the angel's stiff clarion: Go on 55
We're happier than we deserve to be 30
We rein a toboggan down banks 28
Were you scared, or would you like 50
When our baby wakes 48
When your head was high 22
Winter nights he honors us 60
Wrapped in wool, with no other 19

Y

Years after he left a prairie town 36
Yup'ik boys lay 42

www.ingramcontent.com/pod-product-compliance
Lightning Source LLC
Chambersburg PA
CBHW011344090426
42743CB00019B/3433